You Are

Joe Santoro

The Santoro Education
Lifeskills Foundation

**Building Your Social and Emotional
Skills to Enhance Your Life**

ISBN-978-1722635596

ISBN-10 1722635592

What they are saying about Joe's books and videos

I have recommended this book to my family members, teaching friends, and friends who have grandchildren.

I am so glad they turned the videos into a book. I will use the book as a journal.

The lesson on communication improved my marriage.

I found this book to be down to earth and concise and it offered good advice to individuals and business owners.

Joe is deeply dedicated to the goal of early learning and the lessons in this book are very powerful.

Even at 60 years old I've learned something. I purchased the book for my son so he can teach his son.

Politicians should read this book to learn how to relate, and get things done.

This book gave me some simple tips and exercises on how to be successful in life.

I can see myself rereading this book multiple times throughout the years.

Lessons are short but to the point. Each lesson has a tip.

About the Author

Joe Santoro is a successful entrepreneur, a philanthropist, and a man devoted to his family and his fellow Americans. He sometimes refers to himself as the proud owner of a PhD in Life. Over the years, he has used his business success to start two foundations.

The Santoro Educational Lifeskills Foundation (SELF) focuses on helping people become the best they can be. All Children First Foundation is focused on Early Learning.

Over his career, Joe expanded his commercial maintenance business to include commercial real estate development, building construction, and leasing and managing millions of square feet of prime office space.

Joe, along with the New Jersey Chamber of Commerce, also started an education program for building a bridge between business and education, and has worked with schools to help students get a better understanding of the business environment.

His first book, <u>Win the Biggest Game: LIFE</u>, sets the blueprint for how he's approached life and his hope that all kids and their parents are happy with themselves. It offers a path to help all children and their parents become the best they can be.

In his own words

I started my own foundation, Santoro Educational Lifeskills Foundation (SELF) (**SantoroFoundation.org**) to help people become the best they can be. I then started the All Children First Foundation (ACFF) (**ACFFnow.org**). The purpose of this was to start a national movement to get our government to spend our money wisely, and to invest in all our children, rich or poor, by funding early learning resource centers to educate children from birth to 5 and help parents become the best they can be.

I put together this book and the *Alive 2 Thrive* programs primarily to help people. I realize the importance of learning these skills as early as possible. I did not always have these skills. It wasn't until I was in my 30's and had a business employing people that I realized the skills I did not have. I went to seminars, read self-help books, and listened to tapes.

Sure, I turned out okay. But it has taken me years to learn these skills. Knowing the skills and actually carrying them out are two different things. Even today I find myself still working on how to implement skills. I think the main reason is because I learned them later in life.

The skills are teachable. The younger you are when you learn the skills, the better off you will be. I realize people who possess these skills and practice them on a regular basis have the highest possibility of being successful and living a life that is RICH. Joe's definition of rich is:

A RICH person is someone who is healthy, knows who they are, is comfortable in their own skin, is doing what they like, is making enough money to support the lifestyle they desire, and has family and friends who love them and truly want to be with them.

Acknowledgements

I would like to thank all the people in my life, the good and the bad. The good people for supporting my efforts and keeping me grounded. The bad people who are difficult to deal with, because they tested my character and my resilience. If things always work out well, there would be no need to learn these skills.

I would like to thank the people who helped me put this book together:

My wife Kate, who always gives me another perspective on things. She worked with me on reviewing the 36 lessons and keeping them short, sweet and to the point.

David Benzel and his company **Growing Champions for Life** on his collaboration on this project.

Author /Speaker Lindsay Collier, **Amazon.com/author/lindsaycollier**, for helping me rewrite these lessons and put this book together.

I'd like to thank the people who buy the book and pass on this knowledge.

I also give my thanks in advance for those who will be supporting my foundations.

How to Use This Book

For Students and Individuals

The ALIVE2THRIVE program only has one goal; **To empower you with the skills you need to guide your own life's decisions and fulfill your potential.**

Honestly, we are asking a lot from you to achieve this goal. Finishing the lessons takes time and it requires you being open and honest. Whether you are using the program by yourself, with a parent/mentor, or in the classroom, to get the most out of the lessons, it is important that you be emotionally honest about how you are feeling with each lesson.

Overall, the curriculum is introduced in four consecutive modules and is meant to be used in order from start-to-finish.

Each lesson has instructions on how you can use its materials. The program will be more effective if you have a trusted person to work through the lessons, and discuss and share your thoughts. With each lesson there are public and private questions for you to answer. Even if you do not have someone else to work with, it is important that you keep a private lesson diary so you can monitor your progress and build upon what you have learned.

.

For Parents, Teachers, and Mentors

Parents, teachers, and mentors play a key role in the success of the ALIVE2THRIVE program. Here is how you can be involved:

For Parents

The **ALIVE2THRIVE** lessons are also for you. We invite you to use this book's lessons to introduce important discussions with your child.

While it can be difficult to bring up some of the topics covered by this curriculum, the lessons are an easy and effective way for you to begin a long-term conversation about sensitive subjects. We ask the same thing from you as we ask of the teachers using this curriculum – that you equally invest your time, commitment and attention to the process.

The teaching process begins with you. It is crucial that you read the lessons and review the questions before talking with your child. When reviewing the materials, think back to how the lesson might have been relevant to you when you were your child's age and even how it is relevant to you now. Being able to share stories of the lesson's significance will help you get your student to share themselves.

In addition, by your sharing, it shows your own investment in the learning process.

After you have reviewed a lesson's materials, you are prepared to share the lesson and questions with your child. Begin by staying within the guidelines of the handout, public and private questions. However, feel free to let your conversation with your child go beyond the questions in the handout. You know them better than we do. Encourage your child to maintain a conversation diary of all of their private question answers. Let them be the one to decide whether they want to share those answers.

Overall, the curriculum is designed in four modules and is meant to be used in order from start-to-finish. If you find that your child has a particular need, such as working with other students in class, you can start with the *Understanding Others* or the *Relating to Others* modules. No matter which lesson you choose to begin this journey, know that this learning process takes time and requires being open and honest with your child.

For Teachers and Mentors

For teachers and mentors, we invite you to use the **ALIVE2THRIVE** book and lessons to start important discussions with your student/s. While it can be difficult to bring up some of the topics covered by this curriculum, the lessons are an easy and effective way for you to begin a long-term conversation about sensitive subjects. We ask the same thing from you as we ask of the parents using this curriculum – that you equally invest your time, commitment and attention to the process.

The teaching process begins with you. It is crucial that you carefully review the lessons and the questions before talking with your student. When reviewing the materials think back to how the lesson might have been relevant to you when you were your student's age and even how it is relevant to you now. Being able to share stories of the lesson's significance will help you get your student to share themselves. In addition, by your sharing it shows your own investment in the learning process.

After you have reviewed a lesson's materials, you are prepared to share the lesson and questions with your student. Start out by staying within the guidelines of the handout, public and private questions. However, feel free to let your conversation with your student go beyond the questions in the handout. You know them better than we do. Encourage your student to maintain a conversation diary of all of their private question answers. Let them be the one to decide whether they want to share those answers.

Overall, the curriculum is designed in four modules and is meant to be used in order from start-to-finish. If you find that your child has a particular need, such as working with other students in class, you can start with the *Understanding Others* or the *Relating to Others* modules. No matter which lesson you choose to begin this journey, know that this learning process takes time and requires being open and honest with your child.

Keep in Mind

These skills are teachable. The younger you are when you learn the skills, the better off you will be. People who possess these skills and practice them on a regular basis have the highest possibility of being successful and living a life that is RICH. Joe's definition of rich is:

A RICH person is someone who is healthy, knows who they are, is comfortable in their own skin, is doing what they like, is making enough money to support the lifestyle they desire, and has family and friends who love them and truly want to be with them.

Table of Contents

Introduction

What is this workbook about, and what should you expect to get out of it if you do the work?

The book is broken down to 36 very short lessons in four major categories, which I call *The Power of Four*.

1. Knowing Me

Know yourself and be comfortable in your own skin. Learn what you like and dislike. Build your self-esteem.   Believe in yourself.

2. Managing Me

Develop your self-control and handle your impulses and emotions. Be truthful with yourself, and develop better decision-making, critical thinking skills, and directions. Set and achieve your goals.

3. Understanding Others

Develop empathy and understand the emotions, perceptions, and needs of others.

4. Relating to Others

Enhance communications and conversation skills, and enable conflict management, constructive resolutions, teamwork, and collaboration to meet goals. Be able to serve others and meet their needs.

In the **Power of Four** lessons I have purposely kept the lessons short and simple, and to the point. Too often, self-help books go into too many details. And they tell you what to do, but not how to do it.

Each lesson has a single point message along with tips on the best ways to achieve results. At the end of each lesson, there will be two questions to help you start on your journey. Included will be a short motivational saying that will help you remember the lesson.

This book is designed to be a workbook. You can use it by yourself, with others, or in groups. Also, a mentor can use this to help others. It can also be used as a journal.

What will you achieve if you learn the skills? People who know who they are and are comfortable in their own skin normally do better in life. It's hard to pick a partner, or pick a job path if you don't know who you are, what you like, and what you dislike.

You will have good healthy relationships at home and at work if you manage yourself, gain self control, manage your impulses, and learn to be truthful. Understanding others, having empathy, and recognizing people's needs, will enable you to make true friends. Once you understand others, it is easier for you to relate to them. Improving your conversation skills and conflict resolution techniques are useful skills for your personal and business life.

Good leaders, good managers, and good parents possess these skills. Becoming a mommy or daddy is easy. We all manage to figure that out. Being a parent is a lot more difficult. Great parents possess these skills and pass them on to their children. By doing that, we will greatly improve our society.

To parents, teachers, mentors, and anyone who wants to use this book, the lessons are also for you. We invite you to use this book and the free videos to introduce important discussions to your children, students, and family.

While it can be difficult to bring up some of the topics covered in this curriculum, the lessons are an easy and effective way for you to begin a long-term conversation about sensitive subjects. We ask the same thing from you as we ask of the teachers using this curriculum – that you equally invest your time, commitment, and attention to the process.

The teaching process begins with you. It is crucial that you read the lessons and watch the videos before talking with your child or student. When reviewing the materials, think back to how the lesson might have been relevant to you when you were your child's age, and even to how it is relevant to you now. Being able to share stories of the lesson's significance will help you get your student to share themselves.

All profits from this book will go to The Santoro Lifeskills Foundation. This book also has a money back guarantee. If you read this book and do the lessons and feel it has not helped you, your money/donation will be refunded.

Great parents possess these skills and pass them on to their children. By doing that, we improve society.

Part One

Knowing Me

The lessons in the KNOWING ME module seek to empower you with the ability to self-reflect upon "What it Means to be You."

1

Knowing Me

Who Do You THINK *You Are?*

Learning Objective: You will understand various options for defining one's self in our culture and the consequences of each.

One of the most important questions you will ever answer just might be, "Who do you think you are?" I'm not talking about the sarcastic version – "WHO do you think you are?" – but the more honest version like "Who do you THINK you are? "

When you think about yourself as a student, an athlete, a musician, father, husband, employee, or even as a friend, I'm asking you to think about how you define yourself.

There are several options you know. For instance, are you:

- what you have?
- the clothing you wear?
- the toys you own?
- the house you live in?
- the friends you have?
- or the car you drive?

Is that what makes you who you are?

Or, are you what you do, and how well you do it? Do you define yourself by the work you do, the sport you play, the instrument you practice, or the hobby you're in? Is that who you are? Or, are you what others say you are? Do you depend on the opinion of others to determine who you think you are and how much you're worth?

The world is full of people who can't quite figure out who they are or what they're worth. If you really believe that you are what you have, then who are you after you lose what you have? Did you know that approximately 70% of lottery winners go broke within a few years? If that was your story, are you suddenly worthless when you're broke? If you are what you do, who are you once you stop doing it; or who are you on the days you don't do it well?

A famous tennis player couldn't figure out who he was once he retired from tennis because he had only thought of himself as "a famous tennis player." It might be tempting to think that who you are is best explained by what others say about you. Many people work hard at pleasing others and behaving in a way that earns the compliments of their friends. But just think of the emotional roller coaster you're riding from one day to the next as the opinion of others dictates your worth.

So here are the questions again:

How do you define yourself?

_____

_____

_____

Who do you think you are?

_____

_____

_____

Where does your value come from?

_____

_____

_____

Is it a good idea to define yourself by what you have, or what you do, or the opinion of others?

_____

_____

Questions:

1. What is the most important new insight or conclusion you got from this lesson and discussion?

_____

_____

_____

_____

2. If you don't define yourself by what you have, or by what you do, or by the opinions of others, you could say "I am valuable because . . ."

_____

_____

_____

_____

_____

_____

_____

*"A man is rich according to what he is,
not according to what he has."*

2

Knowing Me

Imagine the Ideal You

Learning Objective: You will identify your most desirable behaviors and attitudes.

The " Magic Bead" Principle

Tie a bead to the end of a ten-inch piece of string. Standing perfectly still, get the bead to move in a clock-wise circle using only your mind. When successful, instruct your bead to move in a counter clock-wise direction using only your mind.

Do this while standing first, and later try it while sitting with an elbow resting on a table (which is a little more difficult). It's important to be quiet, focused, and totally concentrating on only the bead. When distracted by other surroundings, the bead will not move – which is a very important learning point.

This exercise illustrates that the mind is such a powerful tool that when we build vivid images of the person we wish to be, our subconscious mind does not judge our vision; it only assumes it to be true. It is based on the fundamental premise that, when we begin with the end in mind, we increase our chances of fulfilling our potential.

Let's apply the "magic bead" principle to your life. Have you ever imagined the ideal vacation, or the ideal summer day? Perhaps you've imagined an ideal performance in your sport, or the perfect job. They say one of the most significant differences between humans and all the animals of the kingdom is our ability to imagine – seeing in the theater of our mind what could be, not just what is.

What if you use your imagination to picture the ideal you? In fact, that's your assignment for today. Use your mind's eye to construct a detailed image of yourself at your very best. It's not necessarily about perfection, and it's certainly not about wishing you were somebody else. It's more about picturing the specific characteristics that shine through when you're at your absolute best.

In 1991, Mike Powell broke the world's long jump record, a record that stood for 23 years. When asked about his performance, he said it felt familiar because he had practiced it in his mind for so many years. He had imagined the exact leap that broke the world's record, and he imagined it in the theater of his mind.

Elite athletes and professional entertainers imagine their ideal performances way in advance. They see every detail and feel every sensation associated with that performance. And that exercise allows the subconscious mind to begin moving them toward their very best.

Why shouldn't you use the same technique to move you toward your very best? Are you ready to imagine the ideal you and put the power of your mind to work?

Discussion:

1. What do you look like physically when you are at your very best?

_____

_____

_____

_____

2. What mood are you in when you are at your very best?

_____

_____

_____

_____

3. What's your attitude about learning something totally new?

_____

_____

_____

_____

4 How does the ideal you react when your work is criticized?

_____

_____

_____

_____

5. What does the ideal you do for a friend in need?

_____

_____

_____

_____

Questions:

1. What benefits will we experience going forward by imagining our ideal self now?

_____

_____

_____

2. Describe the "ideal you" in the following situations.

- When you have to learn something new:

- When your work is criticized:

- When a friend is in need of help:

- When you get bad news about something:

- When you are in your best mood:

_____

_____

_____

_____

_____

_____

"Be the best YOU can be."

3

Knowing Me

Another Kind of Smart

Learning Objective: You will create a personal plan for improving your personal Emotional Quotient (EQ).

This lesson will help you create a personal plan for improving your personal emotional quotient (EQ). By improving your EQ, you will work to close the gap between your current self and your IDEAL self by managing your emotions.

Emotional Quotient

If IQ stands for Intelligence Quotient, what does EQ stand for? The answer – Emotional Quotient. Your EQ refers to how smart you are with your emotions and how well you understand the emotions of others.

It turns out that high EQ is a better predictor of success than IQ. Here's an example:

When 13 year old Natalie Gilbert forgot the words in the middle of the *Star Spangled Banner* at a Portland Trailblazer's game, Maurice Cheeks recognized her embarrassment and stepped up to put his hand on her shoulder, and joined in to help her finish the national anthem (in spite of being a terrible singer). That's high EQ!

On the other hand, when the jockey in the movie *Seabiscuit* thought he had been fouled by another jockey, he totally abandoned his race strategy in order to get revenge. He said, "I've been fouled." In the process he lost a race he could have won. Losing his temper and trying to get even is an example of low EQ.

The good news is that EQ can be improved. It is a *do it yourself project*, but you need a plan. Here's a good approach. Using your "Ideal Self" list from the previous lesson, identify where your everyday self is nearly your ideal self. We'll call these your "strengths." Next, identify where your everyday self is not close to your "Ideal Self." These are your "gaps," and we all have some.

The question is, are you working on your GAPS? Improving the GAPS is one way to increase your EQ. You can close the GAP between the current you and the IDEAL you by managing your emotions.

Here's why it's important:

• 34% of hiring managers are placing greater emphasis on emotional intelligence when hiring and promoting employees.

• 71% value emotional intelligence in an employee more than IQ.

• 59 % of employers would not hire someone who has a high IQ but low EQ.

• For workers being considered for a promotion, the high EQ candidate will beat out the high IQ candidate 75% of the time. So, exactly why did the hiring managers feel emotional intelligence is so important? Those with high EQ excelled at staying calm under pressure, resolving conflict effectively, behaving with empathy, and leading by example.

Here are some tips:

- Pick just one GAP at a time to improve.

- If you're working on being more patient with a family member or fellow employee, practice responding to him or her like someone whose patience you really admire.

- If you're working on being more positive when you get bad news, experiment with some new positive thoughts about the good that's hidden in the bad news.

- Experiment with new ways of handling situations that normally get you upset.

Questions:

1. Think of a recent situation in which you became angry. "My emotional response was to:

_____

_____

_____

_____

_____

What happened because of your anger?

_____

_____

_____

_____

_____

2. If I was acting closer to my ideal self, I would have responded by

_____

_____

_____

_____

_____

What would you have done? What benefits would that get you?

_____

_____

_____

_____

_____

"Emotional intelligence makes you a complete person."

4

Knowing Me

Two Faces of Character

Learning Objective:

You will learn to prioritize your most desired character traits and chart a course for improvement.

We don't have to look very far to find examples of good or poor character traits. We see it in sports, business, and in school. Examples of good character show up in our heroes, and sometimes poor character still ends up holding a trophy at the end of a game. It can be confusing.

Character has two faces. Some character strengths face inward toward self, and some character strengths face outward toward others. This lesson offers a list of both types. You will explore which type of characteristics you possess and how many of these characteristics are about you or your relationship with others.

When it comes to character building strategies, which of the following do you prefer and why?

Writing about it _____

Role playing to try it_____

Talking about it_____

Story telling about it_____

Reading About it_____

Doing it_____

Modeling the way_____

Debating pros and cons_____

Circle What You Consider the Top Ten Most Important Character Strengths

From "The Only Way to Win" by Dr. Jim Loehr

Effort Investment	Seeking Challenges
Perseverance	Resilience
Self Discipline	Self-Control
Constructiveness	Ambition
Optimism	Resourcefulness
Determination	Reliability
Concentration	Positivity
Love for Others	Justice
Care for others	Fairness
Kindness	Curiosity
Honesty	Responsibility
Hope	Competitiveness
Love of learning	Punctuality
Creativity	Decisiveness
Critical Thinking	Mental Toughness
Humor	Bravery
Focus	Patience with Self
Commitment	Diligence
Truthfulness	Loyalty to Others
Integrity	Patience with Others
Humility	Respect for Others
Gratefulness	Honor

Questions:

1. Which three character traits do you choose as most urgent to be improved?

_____

_____

_____

_____

_____

2. Which strategies from page one are the best methods for you to grow your character, and why?

_____

_____

_____

_____

_____

"Our character is what we do when we think no one is looking."

5

Knowing Me

Find Your Swagger

Learning Objective:

You will learn the nature of self-confidence and its source and explore the difference between legitimate swagger and phony arrogance.

Have you noticed that some people seem to have it all together? They look and sound so sure of themselves while you feel like a pair of flip-flops in a world full of Nikes.

What's up with that? Are they faking it, or is that swagger for real? Well, I think there's actually a formula for swagger. I'm not talking about arrogance, but the real genuine kind of poise that's cool without trying to be cool. So here it is...sort of like a math equation. High Self-esteem + High Self-confidence = Major Swagger.

What is self-esteem? Some people think it's walking down the street knowing that your friends like you. That's not bad, but it's more important that you walk down the street knowing that YOU like you – even though you're not perfect. Seriously, do you like you? It would be good for the rest of us if you did. People who like themselves are more fun to be around! So start treating yourself like someone who is likable–because deep down you are!

Next, what is self-confidence? Some people think it's being the best at something. That's not really it. Self-confidence is BELIEVING in your skills. It's believing you can deliver a performance equal to what you've learned so far in them…and that's all.

A coach says the skills you have are only good when you BELIEVE in them. Of course no one has all the skills they need, but once you believe you can LEARN new skills, you can be confident all the time.

Sometimes swagger is just believing you can learn to solve the problem, learn to hit the curve ball, learn to make the moves, or even learn to say the right thing at the right time. So, what do you believe about YOU right now? That's the question. Do you believe in your skills? Do you believe you can learn new ones? Confidence is just believing, and here's why it's so important:

No one ever performs consistently at a level higher than what they believe to be true about themselves.

Come on, it's time to get a little more swagger. Because whether you say, "I can" or you say, "I can't"…either way you're right!

High Self-Esteem (Why do I like me?)

Plus

High Self-Confidence (Which of my skills do I believe in? Or, what do I believe I can learn?)

Equals

SWAGGER (Not arrogance)

Questions:

1. Which of your skills can you count on when needed?
Describe your confidence.

_____

_____

_____

_____

_____

_____

2. What do you imagine true Swagger would feel like for
you?

_____

_____

_____

_____

_____

_____

*"You can only have true Swagger when you have
good self-esteem and confidence."*

6

Knowing Me

So What Do You Expect?

Learning Objective:

You will understand the power of expectations and learn how to identify personal tendencies.

Y ou sit down to take a test. What do you expect the next ten minutes to be like? Satisfying or *crash & burn*? You meet a friend to talk about a disagreement you had with each other over lunch. What do you expect from the conversation, resolution or more hostility? You step up to the plate in a baseball game with a runner on third. What do you expect will happen, an RBI or an out? A customer calls. Do you expect a complaint or something good? This will affect how you answer the call, upbeat or timid.

Some people are in the habit of expecting good things, and some people always expect the worse. Which one are you? Research shows that what you expect has a lot to do with what happens next. Scientists put volunteers in two groups, told them to throw darts at a target, and record the results.

Next, they gave them a personality test. Afterwards the researchers told half the people that the test showed that they're the kind of people who perform well under pressure. The other half were just told they passed the test. Then both groups were challenged to improve their dart throwing accuracy by 15%, and that those who did would be given cash prizes.

90% of those who were told they'd likely do well under pressure hit the accuracy goal, compared to only 27% of the other group. Expecting positive things from yourself improves your chances for success.

DISCUSSION:

The brain is made up of billions of connections (synapses), and the thoughts we have are by-products of patterns of connections. These patterns are uniquely formed for each of us over time as a result of our experiences.

Our positive experiences of fun, joy, peacefulness, comfort, acceptance, forgiveness, and love create thought patterns that affect what we expect.

Our negative experiences of boredom, anxiety, hurt, isolation, blame, and rejection also create patterns that affect what we expect.

Step 1: Become aware of your thought patterns. Observe your thoughts like a witness to an event. Notice the triggers that send your brain into thought production.

Step 2: Keep a record of the kind of thoughts you're having in the various environments you encounter each day. Categorize your thoughts as being either positive or negative in nature.

Step 3: Ask yourself whether your current thoughts are helpful or harmful to your progress. A future lesson will teach you how to change your thoughts!

The first step in improving your expectations is to begin listening to that little voice in your head. Become aware that there is an inner voice. The voice is not you; it's just your brain spitting out thoughts at lightning fast speed – about 60,000 of them a day. Notice whether they are encouraging thoughts with positive expectations, or negative thoughts predicting doom and gloom. Spend a couple of days just observing what your brain is kicking out and keep a record of your thought tendencies. But remember, "*You are not your brain.*"

Questions:

Keep a record of your frequent thoughts below; then decide which ones are most helpful to your progress.

Positive Thoughts: Any thought that encourages me or takes me closer to being my ideal self.

At Work:

_____

_____

_____

_____

With Friends:

_____

_____

_____

_____

At Home:

_____

_____

_____

_____

Negative Thoughts: Any thought that discourages me or takes me farther from being my ideal self.

At Work:

_____
_____
_____
_____

With Friends:

_____
_____
_____
_____

At Home:

_____
_____
_____
_____

"You are what you think."

7

Knowing Me

Choose Optimism

Learning Objective:

You will identify optimistic and pessimistic responses and learn how to benefit from optimistic choices.

So which one are you, a Pessimist or an Optimist? Or are you one of those people who think it doesn't really matter? Well let's define each one first.

Pessimists tend to believe the bad things that happen affect everything in life and are due to being dumb or unlucky. In other words, it's a permanent condition; and it's who they are.

Optimists tend to believe the bad things that happen are temporary blips on the screen-of-life and are due to the mistakes they make, but it's NOT who they are. They know that circumstances can be changed next time around, and they're determined to make an adjustment in the future.

Experiments show that Pessimists tend to give up more quickly, and Optimists tend to do better in life and in sports. Pessimists explain things that happen like this:

"I'm so dumb." "I always make mistakes like that."

Optimists are more likely to say:

"I wasn't thinking on that one." "I'm having an off day."

CONSIDER THESE TRUTHS:

• Some thoughts come from our brain without our permission.

• We can choose to immediately correct or replace a thought.

• Your brain is a tool you've been given to control.

• You are not the mistakes you make.

• Optimistic people have learned to view mistakes as temporary circumstances.

The big news is that Pessimists can learn to be Optimists using a simple skill:

Learn to argue with yourself! When you hear your brain say something like, "I'm so bad at tests," immediately argue back by reminding yourself of the times you've done well. If your brain says, "I always blow it in games," learn to stand up for yourself by pointing out a fact that proves it's not true. "I made a great play last week!" Correct the brain about the lies it tells.

When you learn the skills of non-negative thinking, you'll be more optimistic; and the benefits are huge! Research shows that optimistic people not only win more often; but they are noticeably better under pressure, and better when they have to overcome obstacles. Remember, this kind of thinking is a choice we make. Choose to be an optimistic thinker when bad things happen. Use your brain as a powerful friend, not a devious opponent.

Questions:

1. Pessimistic explanations of mistakes often sound like this:

_____

_____

_____

_____

Sometimes I choose to say…

_____

_____

_____

Optimistic explanations of mistakes often sound like this:

_____

_____

_____

_____

Sometimes I choose to say…

_____

_____

_____

2. A specific argument I need to have with myself is about _____

(Choose an area of your life in which you are often pessimistic.)

When my pessimistic self says…

_____
_____
_____
_____

My optimistic self could say…

_____
_____
_____
_____

"Think negative, get negative. Think positive, get positive and happy."

8

Knowing Me

Win the Biggest Game

Learning Objective: You will understand the role of one's core values and articulate their application in your life.

W e've all heard about the BIG game… or the BIG test… or the BIG job application, …the one that will define our season, or our future. If you win the BIG ONE, you're hot stuff and; if you lose, there is only disappointment and the phrase, "There's always next time."

But what if I told you the BIG game is actually a small event within an even BIGGER game that's going on? What if the BIGGEST game is the one that really deserves your attention? In fact, it's so critical because there is no "Next Time." You only get one shot at this

BIGGEST game. The Biggest game is the game of LIFE, and here's the deal:

It lasts longer, is more important, and has more opponents than a normal competition. The stakes are huge! If you lose this game called LIFE, the lessons are painful, your relationships are all drama, and there's no second place trophy.

In this game, the question is not what are you GETTING, but what are you BECOMING. Yet so many people take their eyes off this game in order to chase little trophies, false friends, and cheap thrills. We're talking about what's REALLY important.

There's nothing wrong with having high recommendations and other successes. But while you're working toward those goals, what kind of marks are you getting on these questions:

- Are you always honest?
- Do you accept responsibility?
- Are you respectful to everyone?
- Are you becoming the kind of person a younger person could look up to?

So while you're running around from job to job, and playing all the little games, check your internal scorecard to see if you're on track to win the most important game of all....**Life!**

A person's core values can be defined as the guiding principles used to make life's decisions. They act like a compass to point the way toward choices and behaviors that are consistent with your sense of right and wrong.

A person committed to their core values will not compromise their actions for convenience, for money, or for popularity. The first step is declaring one's core values. The second step is prioritizing them. The third step is understanding the implications of living up to these principles and "**Walking the Talk**."

Where are you not "Walking your Talk?"

Questions:

1. Circle your top five personal core values and then rank order them.

Accuracy	Health/Fitness
Adventure	Honesty
Appearance	Humor
Authenticity	Independence
Collaborating	Integrity
Commitment	Joy/Fun
Competitiveness	Justice
Creativity	Leadership
Directness	Love/Nurturing
Elegance	Orderliness
Empowerment	Peace/Tranquility
Enthusiasm/Passion	Personal Power
Excellence	Humility
Freedom to choose	Hard work
Growth/Learning	Recognition
Harmony	Resilience

Respectfulness   Success/Achievement

Results   Tradition

Risk Taking   To be Known

Security   Trust

Service   Winning

Spirituality   Vitality/Zest

Sports/Recreation

2. What does the phrase "Losing at Life" mean to you?
What does it look like?

_____

_____

_____

_____

_____

_____

_____

3. In what ways could you do a better job of being true to
your top two core values?

_____

_____

_____

_____

"Life is not a dress rehearsal."

9

Knowing Me

Avoid Self Deception

Learning Objective:

You will understand personal denial and identify examples from your life.

D r. Ignaz Semmelweis delivered babies at Vienna's General Hospital in the mid-1800s. He also had responsibilities doing research on cadavers when he wasn't delivering babies. One in ten women died giving birth in his ward, while a second maternity ward staffed by mid-wives had a much lower mortality rate.

He couldn't figure out why. Then Semmelweis left Vienna for a four-month visit to another hospital. When he returned, he discovered the mortality rate had improved dramatically while he was gone. Suddenly Semmelweis had to ask himself a tough question.

What part did he play in this terrible problem? When he realized that the primary difference between his work and the work of the mid-wives was that he spent extra time working on cadavers, and they did not, Semmelweis developed his theories about the existence of germs. He determined that tiny diseased particles were being carried from the cadavers to the healthy patients on his own hands!

This discovery led to the practice of doctors scrubbing their hands to get rid of germs. But think of how Semmelweis felt when he realized his own contribution to the death rate. The true answer to the problem was found only when he asked the most important question: "What part of this problem is caused by me?"

DISCUSSION:

The questions that follow are designed to help us think of situations in which we played a part in a misunderstanding or conflict, and to honestly admit our role in whatever happened. Answering our own questions honestly works best when we write them down. The first step is to ask each question out loud, and then listen to the internal answer that naturally comes.

Secondly, begin writing so as to record those thoughts that come from within. Writing down our thoughts activates the right hemisphere of the brain and reveals more truth, and less self-denial. We have some really good answers locked inside of us, just waiting for a really good question to be asked.

So ask it! Deception is common, but self-deception is seldom recognized. Have you ever been upset with a situation involving a friend, and then discover YOU caused the problem without realizing it? Everyone likes to be "Right" rather than "Wrong." The problem is that we place such a premium on being "right" that we lose the humility to consider the possibility of being "wrong!"

So, we blame, we finger point, and we excuse ourselves, when instead we should look in the mirror and ask the question, "What part of this situation is mine?" You can minimize these little dramas in all your relationships if you're willing to ask, "What part of this situation is caused by me?"

Questions:

1. In what way did I offend someone, add confusion, or miscommunicate in a recent situation?

_____
_____
_____
_____
_____
_____

2. What benefits will I experience by answering questions like this for myself?

_____
_____
_____
_____
_____
_____

"It's hard to improve if you don't accept responsibility."

Part Two

Managing Me

The MANAGING ME module seeks to empower you with the ability to guide your own thoughts in more positive directions each day.

10

Managing Me

Recovering Self Confidence

Learning Objective:

You will learn how to regain confidence when it is threatened by circumstances.

My name is Tyler, and I've been fortunate enough to play baseball all the way to the professional level. My consistency as a hitter was my strength and got me moved up to varsity as a freshman.

One season I started out pretty well, and then suddenly I couldn't get a hit. For three games I was hopeless. Then

I started to wonder why; and wonder turned to worry; and worry turned to doubt. Two weeks without a hit transformed doubt into real fear. I began to think, "I can't hit anymore." Can you guess what happened next? Yep, another week of ground outs and strike outs.

During this little crisis, my self-confidence took a serious hit. But here's what I learned. Whether it's sports, music, work, or in the classroom, doubt and fear are the true enemies of self-confidence, not the slumps we're in or the actual mistakes we make. Doubt and fear come from the lies we believe about ourselves when things are not going well.

I started to believe a lie about myself, "I can't hit anymore." Once I started to believe that lie, my performance began cooperating with that thought. We get a lot of messages about ourselves every day. We can't control the messages coming from others, but we can control the messages we create about ourselves.

I tried using statements like "I'm so awesome" or "I'm the best," but it was just so phony. Confidence is built on beliefs, so affirmations must be believable! I realized I needed positive self-talk to send positive pictures to my brain, but it had to be truthful...like, "I'm a hard worker," "I'm good at over-coming problems," "I have excellent bat speed." Negative phrases like, "I can't keep up," "I can't hit a curve ball," "I'm so uncoordinated," and "I stink" will sabotage your success;

because the sub-conscious mind believes whatever it hears!

The encouraging messages we say to ourselves open the door to overcoming self-doubt. The more fearless you become, the better you will perform.

By the way, I broke out of my hitting problems by refocusing on all the qualities that made me a good hitter in the first place. Remember, **what you believe with feeling becomes your reality!**

Fear and doubt produce lies that cause us to lose self-confidence. They steal our attention away from other truths we know about ourselves. That's why it's important to identify our personal strengths and stay focused on them, especially when circumstances seem threatening. We are not the mistakes we make! We need to recognize that fear and doubt are the real enemies and that all our true strengths come from our positive affirmations.

Questions:

1. What lies have you told your brain when you've lost self-confidence?

I've heard myself say…

_____

_____

_____

_____

_____

_____

_____

2. What positive things can you tell yourself to regain self-confidence?

I'm the kind of person who…

_____

_____

_____

_____

_____

_____

_____

Read your answers to this question every day.

"Slumps are temporary. If you did it once, you can do it again."

11

Managing Me

Living Above the Land of Excuses

Learning Objective:

You will learn the difference between excuses and personal responsibility, and demonstrate examples.

There's nothing quite so appealing as a good excuse when you've blown it! It sounds like a perfectly logical thing to do. No one likes to pay the price for missing an appointment, making an error, or not getting their chores done.

But have you ever stopped to think how excuses make you sound? There are two reasons why people like to hide behind lame excuses:

1. They're trying to escape the consequences they actually deserve.

2. They want to maintain the illusion of being perfect, even though everyone watching knows the real truth.

Let's look at it this way. With every action taken and every word spoken we choose between living "below the line" of responsibility, in the land of excuses – or living "above the line" of responsibility, where we take personal ownership.

When we learn that those are the only two options, and one of them makes us sound weak, life actually gets easier. When we're below the line we usually offer statements like:

"It's no big deal."

"It's not my fault."

"It's so & so's fault."

"No one told me."

Why does living consistently above the land of excuses take courage and self-discipline? What forces are at work that make it tempting to offer excuses for poor performances and mistakes?

Which of the previous lessons have provided insights that can help you master this concept?

When we live above the line we follow three steps:

- We see things honestly, without lying to ourselves or others.

- We confess it and own it. ("Sorry, my bad – I could have done that better.")

- We take the steps to correct it or prevent it from happening again.

Life is full of opportunities to play the blame game, but just imagine what life would be like if everyone lived above the line and refused to stoop into the land of excuses. What would your life look like if you were to make that choice?

Questions:

1. Why is it hard to avoid making excuses? Why don't people "own up" to their mistakes?

_____

_____

_____

_____

_____

_____

2. Describe the situations where you find it most challenging to own and admit your mistakes.

_____

_____

_____

_____

_____

_____

"Excuses are what you get when you have poor management."

12

Managing Me

The Search for Happiness

Learning Objective:

You will learn strategies for raising your personal happiness set-point.

Do you ever wonder why some people are happier than others? How did they get that way? People at every age and every walk of life list happiness as one of the things they want. Everyone wants to be happy. So most people get busy trying to figure out what will bring them happiness.

They start looking toward their friends, hoping they will make them happy. They buy toys and luxuries, thinking these material things will bring happiness to them. Some people believe their activities will satisfy their need for happiness.

But all of us know people who have a ton of friends, or expensive toys, or lots of activities – and they're still not happy. All of these strategies are based on a common success theory that's a combination of "IF and "THEN."

IF I get a good performance review, THEN I'll be happy. IF I get her to like me, THEN I'll be happy. IF I get an iPhone, THEN I'll be happy. Basically, we believe that IF we achieve success at something, THEN we'll be happy.

So why are so many successful people unhappy? And why are you only temporarily happy when you get a good review, a new phone, or a trophy?

The answer is because the **Success = Happiness** formula is a lie! That's right…success is **NOT** the way to happiness. In fact – let this thought sink in for a minute:

There is no WAY to happiness; Happiness IS the Way.

What does that mean? It means that happiness is a choice people make. It is a way of thinking and acting every single day. Most importantly, success tends to follow happy people, not the other way around. You're more likely to be successful once you decide to be happy!

Over 200 research studies have shown that happiness leads to success in work, school, friendships, sports, business, and marriage. If you're looking for some tips on how to do that, here are five strategies that the researchers at the National Institute for Mental Health discovered:

• Write down three things that went well at the end of every day.

• Be thankful for three things every day, and keep a Gratitude Journal.

• Write a "Forgiveness Letter" to someone, even if you never send it.

• Use an optimistic style of explaining the unfortunate things that happen.

• Set aside time for meditation or reflection daily.

These techniques really work if you do them every day. You'll still have some bummer days, but there's a reason why some people are generally happier than others. They choose to be happy, and everything from their smile to their swagger says so most of the time. The choice is yours. You can choose "unhappy" or you can choose "happy" and enjoy the results!

Questions:

1. Why do people often try to reach happiness through material things?

_____

_____

_____

_____

_____

_____

2. Write some examples of times when you thought "IF I get _____ THEN I'll be happier."

_____

_____

_____

_____

_____

_____

"There is no way to happiness; happiness is the way."

13

Managing Me

The Stories We Tell Ourselves

Learning Objective:

You will identify how circumstances generate personal interpretations and emotional reactions.

There's an old story about a young boy who notices that his grandfather is troubled. "What's wrong grandfather?" asks the boy.

"There's a battle raging within me," says the grandfather, "A battle between an angry resentful wolf and a patient understanding bear." "Who will win?" asked the young boy. The grandfather replied, "It all depends on which one I feed."

The wise grandfather was aware of one of the most important truths about human emotions, and he was trying to teach his grandson a valuable life lesson. Here it is:

1. My feelings come from my thoughts.

2. I think my own thoughts.

3. Therefore. I create my feelings and I'm responsible for them.

Many people fail to grasp this concept. And it's obvious when you hear someone say things like, "My boss/coach makes me mad." or "My mom drives me crazy." or "My boy friend makes me jealous."

In each case a person is claiming that something that happened, – which we'll call "A" – is causing an emotion – which we'll call "C". While it appears that "A" causes "C", the truth is it doesn't actually work that way. It's simply not true.

You can learn to control your emotions if you can remember one little secret. Here's it is:

In between "A" and "C" is a moment...perhaps only a millisecond ... when you tell yourself a story to explain or make sense of the things that happen to you. Let's call that moment "B." The emotions you experience at

"C" depend on what story you tell yourself at "B." In reality, "A" does not cause C. A causes B, and B causes C. Let's look at an example.

When an athlete makes an error in a game, if he FEELS embarrassed, it's probably because the story he told himself was "People are thinking I'm really bad." This kind of story can lead to even more errors as the game goes on. What can he do about this? He can learn to tell himself a better story. After an error, the story could be "I'm better than that; I'll get the next one." which would create an emotion of determination, not embarrassment.

You have a split second after any event when you can choose how to interpret its meaning....whether you're in a game, or walking down the hall when someone ignores you, or comments on how you're dressed. We choose the meaning of every event, by the stories we tell ourselves. You see, it's not what happens to us that matters; it's what we think it means, and how we respond.

Telling ourselves better stories doesn't mean lying to fool ourselves. It means looking for alternative explanations for events that could also be true. With practice, we can learn not to jump to the worst possible interpretation of why other people do and say things.

So, like the boy's grandfather, you get to choose which animal you'll feed every day. Will it be Anger and Resentment, or Patience and Understanding?

Questions:

1. Why do we blame others for the emotions we have?

_____

_____

_____

_____

_____

2. Think of a strong emotion that you felt recently? "I felt very:

_____

_____

_____

_____

_____

3. Identify the event ("A") that happened before the feeling came.

_____

_____

_____

_____

_____

4. What story did you tell yourself about the event?
("B") "I interpreted this event as meaning…

_____

_____

_____

_____

_____

5. Write a new story that could also be true. (New "B")
"I felt very _____."

_____

_____

_____

_____

_____

_____

*"Your Thoughts = Your Feelings = Your Attitude.
You are what you think!"*

14

Managing Me

Don't Feel Like It, Do It Anyway

Learning Objective:

You will learn the meaning of self-discipline and list applications of it in your own life.

B y the time I was 10, I had my tennis goals written down and stuck on my bedroom wall. I was pretty competitive, and I wanted to win some junior tennis tournaments. It takes a ton of practice to be any good.

My dad was supposed to take me to the tennis courts one Saturday morning for some extra practice, but it was a windy and nasty day. After breakfast Dad said he'd load up the car and get ready to drive to the courts. I said, "Dad, I don't really feel like practicing today." He said, "I understand. I'll go get the car ready."

I looked surprised and said again, "It's nasty out there, and I really don't feel like practicing." Again he said, "I know, you're right. I'll go get the car ready." By then I was really frustrated. "Dad! Don't you get it? I don't FEEL like it!"

My dad stopped, looked at me and said, "It's perfectly fine that you don't feel like practicing, but what does that have to do with it? Let's do it anyway."

Now I'm thinking, "Why should I practice when I don't feel like it?" But before I could say it, my dad said something I'll never forget: "It's possible for you to "not feel like it" all the way to a national championship, if you're willing to keep practicing, ESPECIALLY when you don't feel like it! Just DO IT ANYWAY."

Well at first I didn't like the sound of that, but I went to the courts that day and ended up having a great session, in spite of the lousy weather. By the time I got home, I was feeling pretty good about myself and my effort. Okay, I know this sounds weird, but those three words my dad said – **Do It Anyway** – became my little secret weapon.

I noticed that there were lots of times during the week when I didn't feel like doing something. I didn't feel like doing my homework, or loading the dishwasher, and I especially didn't feel like picking up my room. I was always looking for the easiest way to get by.

But then I read somewhere that winners are people who are willing to do what others won't do, so they can have what others don't have. So now whenever I have that feeling of "I don't feel like it" – and I know it's something that's good for me – I just take a deep breath and say those three words – "**Do it anyway,**" and I'm always glad I did. Guess that's why they call it SELF discipline. "Feeling like it" has nothing to do with it!

Questions:

1. What kind of life will a person have by doing only the things he/she feels like doing?

_____

_____

_____

_____

_____

_____

2. Describe two important activities that require your self-discipline and why you should "**Do it anyway**."

_____

_____

_____

_____

_____

_____

"Winners do what losers do not want to do."

15

Managing Me

Illusion of Winning

Learning Objective:

You will understand the benefits of daily progress toward goals and articulate examples.

Not all things are as they appear. For instance, sometimes we pour ourselves into things expecting certain results... only to discover that we were misinformed about where to put our energy.

Let's look at Sarah and what she learned about the illusion of being a winner. Sarah thought winners were people who had tall trophies, shiny medals, and blue ribbons. When she looked at the mantel at her house and saw she didn't have any, she thought she must be a...

well, she didn't want to say the "L" word but she worried that it must be true. The harder she tried to win at anything – work, school, sports, or music – she always came up empty handed.

Then one day her dad suggested that perhaps she was looking in the wrong place and working the wrong way. "What do you mean? I always try hard to win." she said. Her dad replied, "Instead of looking at the mantel and always comparing yourself to others, try looking in the mirror and compare yourself only to you."

Then he gave her a new definition of winning that changed everything. "**Winning is ending each day being a little better than you were that morning**."

• When you perform poorly compared to your best, but still beat the competition, how do you feel?

• When you beat your personal best, but still get beat by others, how do you feel?

• What is more important to you: beating others, or beating your best?

• Which one is most beneficial to you in the long run?

Sarah's dad understood an important truth: If you make a tiny bit of progress every single day, and end that day better than you were that morning, you are winning. And if you are winning, day after day, you must be a winner.

It's all about daily progress. For example, winning could mean preparing for your job better than you did yesterday. It may mean being more patient with your family today than you were yesterday, or being more organized than you were yesterday. Perhaps it means improving your performance in your favorite sport.

It's always about competing with yourself…with YOUR previous best. What the world calls winning is actually the inevitable outcome of beating your own personal best day after day. And a trophy is just a symbol of your victory over self-doubt, fear, and laziness.

Sarah liked the idea of competing against herself. She believed she could beat her best over and over again, and then she'd let the trophies just show up on their own.

Take the pressure off yourself. Instead of comparing yourself to others, focus on ending each day a little better than you were that morning in some area of your life. You'll feel like a winner every day!

Questions:

1. Why do we compare ourselves and our performances to other people so often?

_____
_____
_____
_____

2. What would be the benefits of comparing yourself to your best instead of to other peoples' best?

_____
_____
_____
_____

3. Name two specific areas of your life in which you'd like to make daily progress and why.

_____
_____
_____
_____

"You only fail when you stop trying."

16

Managing Me

Look Good or Learn More

Learning Objective:

You will learn the difference between effort and talent and how they each impact performance.

Research at Stanford University revealed that people tend to fall into one of two categories when it comes to reacting to mistakes. We're going to call these two groups the *Look Good Mindset* and the *Learn More Mindset.*

The *Look Good* group believes "you either have talent or you don't." So they try to "look good" at what they do, even if it means avoiding a tough opponent. If you're in this group you probably stay away from really difficult challenges. You won't run a race against someone you think is faster.

The *Learn More group* believes they are CAPABLE of improving WHATEVER talent they have AS LONG as they keep working at it. They strive to "learn more" by tackling difficult tasks, even if it makes them look less skilled at the moment. They view mistakes as stepping stones to getting better. If you're in this group, you aren't worried about facing a tough opponent; because you assume you can learn from it.

Why are we so afraid that others might discover our weaknesses or areas where we lack knowledge? How can we get over this fear so we can be free to learn or develop new skills?

The key difference between these two mindsets is that the *Look Good group* avoids opportunities where mistakes might be made, while the *Learn More group* pushes personal limits and gives mistakes a GREAT BIG HUG!

If you'd like to join the *Learn More* mindset, here's how to do it.

• Say goodbye to your ego that wants to "look" talented, and replace it with a curiosity for learning new skills.

• Invest your energy in LEARNING every chance you get. Act like a SPONGE and soak up new information that comes your way.

. • Welcome any mistake AS PART of the learning process. See it as a sign that you are learning what works -- and what doesn't work.

Now, take a look at who made a TON of mistakes on their WAY to success!

Henry Ford: His early businesses failed and left him broke five times before he founded the successful Ford Motor Company.

Thomas Edison: Teachers told Edison he was "too stupid to learn anything." He made 1,000 unsuccessful attempts at inventing the light bulb.

Walt Disney: He was fired by a newspaper editor because they said he "lacked imagination and had no good ideas."

What are you into...Looking Good OR Learning More?

DISCUSSION:

Why are we so afraid that others might discover our
weaknesses or areas where we lack knowledge?

_____

_____

_____

_____

_____

_____

How can we get over this fear so we can be free to learn
or develop new skills?

_____

_____

_____

_____

_____

_____

Questions:

1. Why do some people prefer to "look good" rather than "learn more" when trying new things?

_____

_____

_____

_____

_____

_____

2. In what specific area of your life are you ready to learn as much as possible, regardless of how you look?

_____

_____

_____

_____

_____

_____

"Nothing in life is to be feared - simply understood."

17

Managing Me

What's the Performance Formula?

Learning Objective:

You will know the individual elements of performance success and how to respond to unsuccessful performances.

M ost people want to perform well, whether it's in work, school, sports, or music. If we could analyze a performance and break it down into a formula, what would we find? What are the elements that make up success? It might be simpler than you think.

Your talent is the first ingredient. And talents are like playing cards. Everyone has been dealt some talent cards, but no one has the whole deck. You can expand your talent if you're willing to look for the second ingredient – Strategies.

Strategies are methods of doing something, including the effort you put in to get it done. The practice you put in actually grows your talent into skills.

The third ingredient is the Belief you have in yourself – your self-confidence. It's whether you believe you can do something, or believe you can't.

Now we draw a line under these three things and add them up like a math problem to find the sum of our talent, our strategies, and our self-belief. Here's the fun part. If all the ingredients are right, it adds up to SUCCESS.

But sometimes adding these things together doesn't equal success. You might be tempted to call this FAILURE. But in reality there's no such thing as failure…there are only LESSONS. And lessons are just delayed success, not failure!

When this happens, some people get very discouraged. They believe their talent is fixed and they can't get any more, so What's the use? The truth is, talent can be grown and success can be reached IF you're willing to adjust your strategy and your effort.

There's nothing wrong with you…it's the strategy you're using. Find a new strategy and try again. With the right kind of strategy and effort, your talents can be transformed into learned skills that equal success. Remember, there's no such thing as failure…only lessons! What lessons are you learning?

DISCUSSION:

Why do many people first question their talent, instead of their strategies or effort, when they have an unsuccessful performance?

_____
_____
_____
_____
_____

What are some of the resources we have when we need to find new and creative strategies that are not obvious?

_____
_____
_____
_____
_____

Questions:

1. Why is it important to view life's setbacks as "lessons" rather than as failures"?

_____

_____

_____

_____

_____

2. Write about an example in which you thought you failed and describe the real lesson you were meant to learn.

_____

_____

_____

_____

The 5 P's: "Proper planning prevents poor performance."

18

Managing Me

Prisoner, Settler, or Pioneer?

Learning Objective:

You will learn three possible responses to adversity and apply them to their personal experiences.

Adversity: "A state of hardship, affliction or misfortune." **Success**: "The degree to which one moves forward despite all adversity."

Have you ever watched a cycling race, like the Tour de France? Man, can those guys fly when they're going down a hill or riding a tail wind – 40, 50, or even 60 miles an hour!

But the real test of a good cyclist is how well they ride going uphill, or against a strong head wind. In fact, that's how they train. They look for hills to climb, and head winds to fight... because that's what makes them strong and gives them endurance for the real test on race day.

It's really the same for all of us. Adversity makes us stronger, when we battle through it. But not everyone chooses to embrace their obstacles or welcome adversity. In fact, many of us whine, complain, and run the other way when things get tough or ugly. It seems like we fall into one of three categories when it comes to handling adversity.

First, there are a lot of "**Prisoners**" out there. They're the ones who give up and say, "It's no use." It's impossible." and "I quit." They're controlled by their circumstances and their anger.

Next we have the "**Settlers.**" They say things like, "This isn't fair." or, "This is as good as I can do." or "This is good enough." They always search for what's comfortable, not for what's best.

But then there are the "**Pioneers**" who stand above their circumstances and say things like, "I can find a way." "I choose to fight." and "I believe it's possible." They almost say, "I love a challenge...bring on the problems!"

Pioneer thinking is different from Prisoner and Settler thinking, and anyone can do it. The next time you run into any kind of adversity, try these three things:

First, look for the lesson – there's something to learn that will take you over, around, or through your problem.

Second, reconsider any assumptions you've made about what can and can't be done. Some walls aren't walls at all once you take a closer look.

Lastly, be willing to change your present strategies to get different results. If you keep doing what you've always done, you'll keep getting what you've always gotten. The biggest difference is that Pioneer thinking sees adversity as an opportunity, not a threat.

So learn to say this out loud today: "**Thanks for the problems....I need the practice!**"

DISCUSSION:

1. Why do people seldom choose Pioneer Thinking when faced with adversity?

_____

_____

_____

_____

_____

_____

2. What are the benefits of Pioneer Thinking?

_____
_____
_____
_____
_____
_____

3. How do you feel after seeing or hearing about people who overcame great adversity?

_____
_____
_____
_____
_____
_____

Questions:

1. What is an example that you've seen of someone overcoming great adversity?

_____
_____
_____
_____
_____
_____
_____

2. What adversity are you facing now, and what would Pioneer Thinking look and sound like?

_____
_____
_____
_____
_____
_____
_____

"Quitting is not an option."

19

Managing Me

Make Your Movie

Learning Objective:

You will learn a proactive strategy for handling discouragement when faced with a learning plateau.

Have you ever been so discouraged about your progress that you just felt like quitting? You know, like when you keep trying but don't get anywhere...so what's the use? I recall a story that a friend once told me about his daughter.

She told him that's where she was with her science class. It seemed like no matter how hard she tried, her grade was near the bottom. She just couldn't get it! And it wasn't because she hated science. It was just hard for her. Here's the really weird part – she wanted to go to nursing school after high school, and you need decent science grades to get in.

One day she told her mom, "That's it! No more science classes for me. I quit. I'll just have to do something else after high school." She expected her to freak, but she didn't. Instead her mother looked at her and said, "Well, it's your story, and you can write the script anyway you want to."

"What do you mean?" asked the daughter listening intently.

"Your story could go like this: Emily wanted to be a nurse, but she got discouraged because of science classes; so she gave up and decided to be something else. OR, it could go like this: Emily wanted to be a nurse AND she got discouraged because of science classes, so she decided to get creative about it. She got some help from an older student who was good at science. She devoted extra time to her science homework so she didn't get behind. She even moved to a desk in the front row of class. Her grades got better and better. Her confidence grew about all that science stuff and she eventually went on to nursing school." "Since it's your story, how do YOU want it to go?"

"I guess my story is like a movie where I'm the script writer, producer, director, and ticket taker to my movie. I get to choose how I want my story to go. I might not get everything exactly the way I want it, but I'll come a lot closer by treating it like it's my movie, and not somebody else's. The big lesson for me was to take control of my movie so I can be the director and the star of my story, and not one of the extras!"

What story are you working on right now? If you're discouraged, I suggest you figure out a twist in the plot that keeps you in a starring role. But don't give up on your own movie!

DISCUSSION:

1. What happens inside us when we imagine things not going well, or never reaching our goal?

_____

_____

_____

_____

_____

2. What do script writers, movie directors and actors do first before shooting a great story?

_____

_____

_____

_____

_____

3. In addition to deciding how you want your "movie" to go, what else will you need to do to make sure it happens?

_____

_____

_____

_____

_____

Questions:

1. Share an example of a time when you have been discouraged about your progress.

_____
_____
_____
_____
_____
_____

2. What part of your story are you working on right now? What are you willing to do to make it come true?

_____
_____
_____
_____
_____
_____

"It's your life. You don't get a second chance."

20

Managing Me

Solve the Mystery of Motivation

Learning Objective:

You will identify the personal unmet needs that fuel your efforts in various life activities.

Motivation is pursuing something you want or need. The more you want it, the harder you will work. There are various levels of motivation: low, medium, and high -- not just "on" or "off." Do you think you can make someone want or need something because you want them to?

Let's take a look at some key questions to help us solve the mystery of motivation:

What is motivation?

_____

_____

_____

_____

_____

How do you get yourself motivated?

_____

_____

_____

_____

_____

When is it hard to get motivated?

_____

_____

_____

_____

_____

When are you really motivated?

_____

_____

_____

_____

_____

How do you motivate someone?

_____

_____

_____

_____

_____

Questions:

1. How can you tell that someone is highly motivated? List three ways!

_____

_____

_____

_____

_____

_____

_____

2. In what area of your life do you wish you had a higher level of motivation, and why?

_____

_____

_____

_____

_____

_____

_____

"If you want something, don't wait. The time will never be better."

21

Managing Me

Ask Wonder-FULL Questions

Learning Objective:

You will articulate specific questions that generate creative solutions to everyday situations.

Have you ever heard yourself ask these things when you're frustrated with yourself or your self-performance? "Why am I such a klutz? Why do I do such dumb things? Why am I never getting anywhere?

What you probably didn't know is that questions like these are actually bad for you. It's a lot like playing ping pong with your brain. Serve up a lousy question, and you'll get a lousy answer back. Your brain is designed to give you answers, and the better the question, the better the answer.

If you ask yourself a question like, "Why do I do such dumb things?" your brain kicks into gear to find an answer; and it's never positive. You just end up focusing on your weaknesses.

It's better to ask questions that begin with "I wonder how I can…." These are called "wonder-FULL" questions, because they fill your brain with wonder; and to "wonder" is what our brains are made to do.

It's like this: If you ask yourself, "I wonder how I can perform better in my job?" your brain will give you different answers than if you ask, "Why do I stink at this job?" An athlete who asks, "I wonder how I can get more arc on my free-throws?" will get different answers than a player who asks, "Why am I blowing it at the free-throw line?"

Think of it this way: You're on a journey to become something more than you are, and NOTHING impacts the direction of your journey more than the questions you ask yourself. So starting today; ask yourself questions that start with "I wonder how I can…" and watch how your brain sends you in a positive direction.

DISCUSSION:

1. Where, or from whom, did we learn to ask ourselves questions like, "Why am I so _____?

_____

_____

_____

_____

_____

2. Questions can pop into our head very quickly...even before we can think carefully about what to ask. What can a person do after asking a lousy question to change the brain's direction?

_____

_____

_____

_____

_____

3. How can we get in the habit of asking Wonder-FULL questions more often?

_____

_____

_____

_____

_____

Questions:

1. Share an example of a negative or "lousy" question you've heard yourself ask your brain.

_____

_____

_____

_____

2. What wonder-FULL questions do you need to ask yourself right now?

_____

_____

_____

_____

Finish this sentence: "I wonder how I can…

_____

_____

_____

_____

"What you say you will believe. Say positive be Positive."

22

Managing Me

Fake It Until You Make It

Learning Objective:

You will learn how to use your body to impact your mental mindset in two minutes.

A young tennis player walked to the parking lot after losing his match in straight sets and threw his gear in the trunk. "I think I should quit this lousy game," he muttered.

Just then an old grey-haired coach walked up and asked, "How was your match?"

"It was awful... I should take up basket weaving." The coach had a newspaper rolled up under his arm and asked the young player this question: "What if I told you I have an advanced copy of next week's paper and it says here in the sports section that you won next weekend's tournament... how would you feel right now?"

"I'd be excited said the boy!"

"Exactly" said the coach. "What would you think about today's loss?"

"Well, I'd just blow it off as a lesson learned."

"Exactly", said the coach. "And how would you feel about tomorrow's practice session?"

"I'd be fired-up and ready to go, and I'd be there early!"

"Exactly" said the coach. "Now, act the way you want to become until you become the way you act."

"You mean I should fake it until I make it?" said the boy.

"Exactly!" said the coach.

Most people understand that our brains affect our bodies. But does it work the other way around? The answer is YES! When you are confident and assertive, your testosterone level is high, and the stress hormone called Cortisol is low. When you are insecure or stressed, they both move in the opposite direction; and that's why your performance suffers.

Here's the important part. When we purposefully put our body into a strong powerful posture that expands our physical size, our testosterone increases and our cortisol decreases automatically. When we display weak powerless body postures that shrink our physical size, our hormones move in the opposite direction.

In fact, standing in the Superman or Superwoman position for as little as two minutes can significantly increase your confidence level because of the resulting chemical shift in testosterone and cortisol. It just doesn't pay to act small! With a little privacy – and two minutes of time, you can use your body to act the way you want to become and increase your chances of performing confidently – in sports, work, and school. And the really good news is that if you do that daily, the newspaper article the old coach had under his arm can become a reality for you.

"Act the way you want to become until you become the way you act."

DISCUSSION:

1. Can you change your mood or confidence by changing your body?

_____

_____

_____

2. How does the way you "carry yourself" affect your confidence or mood?

_____
_____
_____
_____
_____

3. Can you think of any animals that enlarge their physical size in an attempt to show power or dominance?

_____
_____
_____
_____
_____

Questions:

1. "It just doesn't pay to act small." What does that mean to you? Give examples.

_____

_____

_____

_____

_____

_____

_____

2. In what situations would you benefit by acting the way you want to become in order to become the way you act?

_____

_____

_____

_____

_____

_____

_____

"If you look and act the part; you can be the part."

Part Three

Understanding Others

The UNDERSTANDING OTHERS module seeks to help you better understand and connect with people who possess different kinds of personality traits.

23

Understanding Others

Connecting With People

Learning Objective:

You will learn the four behavioral styles, and how they appear to others.

Knowing how to connect with people is an important skill. And you've got to have their number. Let's talk about connectivity, that human chemistry that, when we have it, we know exactly when we have connected with someone. It feels good. We might say, "We really hit it off," or "We just clicked," or "We're very close."

We're referring to some kind of synergy or chemistry between two people that really feels good and means, "I understand you." We know when it's there, and we know when it's missing.

When you understand someone more, you are more accepting of their behaviors; and therefore they are more comfortable with you. Some people appear weird. But they are really not weird; they just behave differently than you. And we know there are all sorts of behaviors out there, and sometimes you think you are the only normal one. The question is, can you take the time to seek first to understand, and then be understood?

The perfect metaphor for this is an iceberg. Two thirds of the iceberg is below the surface, and only one third is the behavior we see in others. So what's below the surface?

Let's talk about the basic difference in our styles. First of all, some people are very outgoing and very assertive; and other people are more reserved and less assertive.

Another way in which we are different has to do with whether we focus on tasks and hide our emotions, or whether we are more focused on relationships and we show our emotions.

So now if we look at these possible combinations and we combine them, we see that actually there are four very distinct styles; and you fall somewhere in this mix. You are a little bit of all of them, but have a distinctive style.

If you are out-going and task oriented, you are more like a **Rhino**. If you are outgoing and relationship oriented, you are more like a **Peacock**. If you are reserved and relationship oriented, we call you the **Retriever**. And our **Owls** are those people who are task oriented and more reserved.

Everyone is somewhere in the mix, but you have a style that is primarily your dominant style.

So, which one are you? You're probably thinking right now that you are a rhino, a peacock, a retriever, or an owl. You are a little bit of all of them, and it's not a matter of being good or bad. The truth is that none of these are good or bad; they're just different.

In the next few lessons you will learn how to connect with each of these. For now, just think of which one is more like you.

Here is a summary of behaviors you might observe in each of the four styles:

An outgoing/more assertive person:

- Talks more
- Talks faster
- Talks louder
- Uses hands more
- Has direct eye contact

A reserved/less assertive person:

- Talks less
- Talks slower
- Talks softer
- Has relaxed hands
- Has indirect eye contact

A task oriented person:

- Has a monotone voice
- Focuses on chores
- Relies on facts
- Has a controlled facial expression

A relationship oriented person:

- Has an inflection in voice
- Focuses on people
- Relies on opinions
- Has animated facial expression

DISCUSSION:

To "connect" with someone means to understand and feel comfortable with them.

1. Why is it beneficial to "connect" with others?

_____

_____

_____

_____

_____

2. Why do you think you have more difficulty "connecting" with some people than with others?

_____

_____

_____

_____

_____

Questions:

1. Which of the four styles is most like you the majority of the time?

_____

_____

_____

_____

_____

2. With which of the four styles do you have the most difficulty connecting? (feeling comfortable with them)

_____

_____

_____

_____

_____

"Accept people, then they will accept you."

24

Understanding Others

Connecting With Rhinos

Learning Objective:

You will learn to understand the motives and preferences of Rhino behavior, and how to adapt to it.

In the last lesson we learned that there are four behavioral styles – Rhinos, Peacocks. Retrievers, and Owls. We are a combination of these styles, but we have a favorite. We have a dominant style.

Let's look at connecting with Rhinos. Some of us are more like Rhinos, and some of are not. But we need to know how to connect with Rhinos so we can have a good relationship with them.

What makes a Rhino tick? They are very outgoing and very task oriented. That means they talk fast, walk fast, and move fast. They like to make decisions, and they like to get things done. They're always in control, and they like to exert power.

What would be the perfect car for a Rhino? A Hummer, of course, because it dominates, and is powerful.

Here's what you can do to connect with a Rhino:

- Get to the point.
- Give them options.
- Compliment them on their accomplishments.
- If you are in a conflict, bring your facts, not your feelings. Rhinos make decisions based on facts.

If YOU are a Rhino, become more "connectable" by:

- Develop more positive patience with others.
- Tone down your bossy-ness.
- Ask more questions.
- Work on your friendliness.

So whether you are a Peacock, a Retriever, or an Owl, it's possible to connect with Rhinos. All we have to do is to move towards them with our own behavioral style. We don't have to give up our own personalities. But if we act a little bit more like a Rhino, they tend to feel more comfortable around us.

So the question is, "Are you willing to adjust your style to make it easier for a Rhino to connect with you?"

DISCUSSION:

To "connect" with Rhinos means to understand and feel comfortable with them to a similar degree that they experience the same thing with you.

1. What's important to understand about the way Rhinos think?

_____
_____
_____
_____
_____
_____

2. Why do you think some people have difficulty "connecting" with Rhinos?

_____
_____
_____
_____
_____
_____

Questions:

1. What are the strengths of people who have Rhino qualities? What are they good at?

_____

_____

_____

_____

_____

_____

2. What could you do better that would help you connect with a Rhino you know?

_____

_____

_____

_____

_____

_____

"All men put their pants on one leg at a time."

25

Understanding Others

Connecting With Peacocks

Learning Objective:

You will learn to understand the motives and preferences of Peacock behavior and how to adapt to it.

Now that you know how to connect with Rhinos, it's time to take a look at another style — connecting with Peacocks. Understanding a style starts with knowing what you are. Some of you are Peacocks. But some of you are not like Peacocks, but want to learn how to connect with them so you can improve your relationships with them.

So let's review how Peacocks see the world. First of all, we know they are very outgoing. And secondly, they are relationship oriented. They want to be around people. People are more important to them than tasks and chores.

In fact, Peacocks most often want to work in a group. They don't like to work alone. They like to receive attention and influence others.

And what would be the perfect car for a Peacock to drive? Of course, something that gets a lot of attention, like a red Corvette. It just screams, "Look at me!"

Let's summarize what you can do to connect with a Peacock.

- Be sociable and friendly.

- Give them variety in their day.

- Compliment them on how they look.

- Have fun and go with the flow.

Peacocks are very easy going.

If YOU are a peacock and want to become more "connectable":

- Listen more carefully to what people say and need.

- Become more organized.

- Provide more details.

- Pay attention to facts.

So whether you are a Rhino, a Retriever, or possibly an Owl, it's possible to connect with a Peacock if you are willing to adjust your style to adapt. You don't have to become a Peacock; you just have to become more like one. And that makes a Peacock more comfortable when they're around you.

Can you adjust your style to make it easier for a Peacock to connect with you?

DISCUSSION:

To "connect" with Peacocks means to understand and feel comfortable with them to a similar degree that they experience the same thing with you.

1. What's important to understand about the way Peacocks think?

_____

_____

_____

_____

_____

_____

2. Why do you think some people have difficulty "connecting" with Peacocks?

_____

_____

_____

_____

_____

_____

Questions:

1. What are the strengths of people who have Peacock qualities? What are they good at?

_____

_____

_____

_____

_____

2. What could you do better that would help you connect with a Peacock you know?

_____

_____

_____

_____

_____

"Learning to accept is the beginning of understanding."

26

Understanding Others

Connecting With Retrievers

Learning Objective:

You will learn to understand the motives and preferences of Retriever behavior and how to adapt to it.

This lesson is all about connecting with Retrievers. Some of you have a behavioral style much like a Retriever, but many of you do not. But perhaps you have a friend or family member who is a Retriever, and you want to learn how to connect with them.

So, the first thing you must do is to understand how they see the world. Retrievers, of course, are reserved; and they are all relationship oriented. That means they love to have people around them. They like to have friends who are very loyal. They avoid conflict because they just want to get along.

Because they want to be liked and keep things steady, what would be the perfect car for a Retriever? Well, something that would allow them to bring their friends along. Something like a passenger van.

Let's look at the strategies for connecting with a Retriever:

- Be sociable and friendly.

- Give them a sense of security.

- Avoid conflict or radical change.

- Have a plan, and stick to it.

These are the kinds of things that make a Retriever comfortable when they are around you.

Now if YOU are a Retriever, and you want to become more connectable:

- Say what you need.

- Be open to change.

- Be more decisive.

- Pay attention to the facts.

So it doesn't really matter whether you're a Rhino, Owl, or Peacock, it's possible to connect with a Retriever if you are willing to adjust your style. You don't have to change who you are. Just move a little closer to what a Retriever's behavior is like, and they will feel more comfortable with you.

Can you adjust your style to make it easier for a Retriever to connect with you?

DISCUSSION:

To "connect" with Retrievers means to understand and feel comfortable with them to a similar degree that they experience the same thing with you.

1. What's important to understand about the way Retrievers think?

_____

_____

_____

_____

_____

2. Why do you think some people have difficulty "connecting" with Retrievers?

_____

_____

_____

_____

_____

Questions:

1. What are the strengths of people who have Retriever qualities?   What are they good at?

_____

_____

_____

_____

_____

2. What could you do better that would help you connect with a Retriever you know?

_____

_____

_____

_____

_____

"Learn to give him one minute of praise."

27

Understanding Others

Connecting With Owls

Learning Objective:

You will learn to understand the motives and preferences of Owl behavior and how to adapt to it.

Now let's take a look at the final style, connecting with Owls. Some of you behave like Owls, and others of you don't; but it is important to connect with Owls. You probably have a friend or family member who is an Owl, and you want to learn how to connect with them and make them more comfortable when you are around them.

To understand Owls, we need to remember that they are very reserved, and they are always task oriented. That means it's important to get the chores done, and to do things right. They take great pride in their accuracy and efficiency.

What is the perfect car for an Owl, since he wants to be accurate and efficient? Well, it's probably a hybrid, maybe a Prius hybrid since it's so practical.

So let's review the strategies for improving our relationship with Owls:

- Be more serious when it's time to get the work done.

- Give them the facts they need.

- Avoid carelessness or risk taking.

- Have lots of details. Owls love details.

If YOU are an Owl and want to become more connectable:

- Lighten up.

- Be open to change.

- Be a little more spontaneous.

- Make decisions more quickly to keep the ball rolling.

So it doesn't really matter if you're a Rhino, or a Peacock, or even a Retriever. It's possible to connect with an Owl if you are willing to adjust your style and adapt to the fact that Owls have different needs and behave differently. Just move a little closer toward them. Don't give up your own style or change who you are; just adjust.

So the question is, "Can you adjust your style to make it easier for Owls to connect with you?"

DISCUSSION:

To "connect" with Owls means to understand and feel comfortable with them to a similar degree that they experience the same thing with you.

1. What's important to understand about the way Owls think?

_____

_____

_____

_____

2. Why do you think some people have difficulty "connecting" with Owls?

_____

_____

_____

_____

Remember: Everyone is a combination of all four styles, but they usually have a dominant style.

Questions:

1. What are the strengths of people who have Owl qualities? What are they good at?

_____
_____
_____
_____
_____
_____

2. What could you do better that would help you connect with an Owl you know?

_____
_____
_____
_____
_____
_____

"Don't judge without walking in another's shoes."

28

The Best Kept Secret to Friendship

Learning Objective:

You will learn and identify the difference between judgment vs. learning responses to the behaviors of others.

E veryone needs friends. It's our nature to be in relationships. But why is it easier for some people to make friends?

Certainly your friends like you. However, your friends also like the way they feel about themselves when they're with you. We don't feel good about ourselves when there's a lack of acceptance. This is usually caused by a lack of understanding, which means we don't know enough about each other.

The first step is to LEARN more about each other. This helps us UNDERSTAND each other which leads to ACCEPTANCE…the foundation of friendship. This sort of thing happens every day. Here are some examples: You're cruising through your day when someone makes a negative comment about a friend of yours. You have a split second to decide between: Judging (You're a jerk!) or Learning (Why would you say something like that?)

You're sitting at home watching TV, and your partner starts making so much noise that you can't hear the TV. You have two choices: To Judge: (You're so mean!) or To Learn: (I'm having trouble hearing the TV…What are you into right now?)

You see someone at a store who dresses very differently than you. Which way does your mind jump: Judging (What a weirdo!) or Learning (I wonder what that person is really like?)

There's a work associate who seems super smart. Do you jump to a judgment? (What a nerd.) or do you want to learn more about her? (Tell me why you like this class so much.)

Every person you know has a story to tell…either about the moment….or about their view of life. The more you learn about them, the more you will understand them; and then, the more accepting you will become. You can have all the friends you need as soon as you replace your Judging with Learning with Understanding, and Accepting others the way they are. This can be reduced down to a simple secret:

Spend more time being INTERESTED than INTERESTING.

DISCUSSION:

1. Describe what it's like to have a really good friend.

_____
_____
_____
_____
_____
_____

2. What's involved in turning someone into a best friend?

_____
_____
_____
_____
_____
_____

3. Learning, Understanding, Accepting – which one of these is most challenging for you and why?

Questions:

1. Thinking about the words, "Spend more time being interested than interesting," what are some ways to do this sincerely?

_____
_____
_____
_____
_____

2. What specific person would you like to have as a friend? What are your next steps for making that possible?

_____
_____
_____
_____
_____

"Friends love you for who you are, not what you have."

Part Four

Relating To Others

The Relating To Others module seeks to make you ready to build stronger friendships, as well as meet the needs of others.

29

Relating To Others

Using Force vs. Power

Learning Objective:

You will understand motives and choices associated with the use of Force vs Power in relationships.

People fall into one of two groups when it comes to getting what they want.

Group 1: Using FORCE to make things happen

Group 2: Using PERSONAL POWER to attract things into existence

- You can make threats, or you can make invitations.

• You can make selfish demands or you can make reasonable requests.

• You can try to control others, or you can try to inspire others.

• You can use anger to make your point or you can use an explanation to persuade.

• You manipulate people, or you can cooperate with people.

• You can yell to be heard, or you can whisper to create listening.

So, which kind of person are you?

Are you like a storm, using FORCE to make things happen; or are you like the power of sunlight, attracting good things to you?

BEHAVIORS OF FORCE

- Ridicule
- Control Punish
- Manipulate
- Criticize
- Blame
- Nag

BEHAVIORS OF POWER

- Support
- Encourage
- Love
- Forgive
- Trust
- Accept
- Listen

DISCUSSION:

1. When it comes to getting what we want, we choose between two approaches: FORCE (to coerce, push, control) or POWER (to attract, draw-in, entice). Which one is your most natural approach to getting what you want?

_____
_____
_____
_____

3. When you think of world history and various forms of government, name a type of government or a country that has relied on each one of these two philosophies.

_____

_____

_____

_____

_____

4. What happens to our relationships as a result of each approach?

_____

_____

_____

_____

_____

Questions:

1. Which approach is used by "bullies," and what are they trying to get? What's wrong with this approach?

_____
_____
_____
_____
_____
_____

2. In what situations would you benefit from using more personal POWER and less FORCE to get what you want?

_____
_____
_____
_____
_____
_____

"You can't lift people up by putting them down."

30

Relating To Others

How To Lose Friends and Alienate People

Learning Objective:

You will learn to identify the behaviors and learn the consequences of fear and pride in relationships.

No one WANTS to be a Turn Off to their friends, but it can happen to any of us. Have you ever wondered what causes people to drift off or actually run the other way? It's usually when we act out of fear, or out of pride.

Here's what I mean. When we're fearful, we're all about protecting ourselves; so we make excuses because we're afraid others won't forgive our mistakes. We blame others because we're afraid we'll look bad for a bad performance. We don't give 100% of ourselves because we're afraid it still won't be good enough.

When we're prideful, we're all about promoting ourselves; so we brag about our performances to make ourselves sound superior. We put ourselves ahead of others because we think we deserve more. We talk about ourselves to impress other people.

All of these are Credibility killers. What is Credibility? It's how much others believe in you and trust you. It's sort of like having "credits" with people. The more credits you've earned by being REAL, the more Credibility you have. If you're dishonest, or a bully, you're going to lose your "credits" in a hurry. Pretty soon…zero Credibility, equals zero Friends!

Here's the funny part. The most credible people on the planet are the ones who spend more time giving credits to others than trying to get them! They praise others instead of themselves. They take responsibility when they mess up. And they offer to play a supporting role if necessary. These are people with REAL humility and REAL Credibility.

Do you have the courage to be REAL instead of fearful? REAL, instead of prideful?

DISCUSSION:

1. What causes us to lose friendships?

_____
_____
_____
_____

2. When we are at our worst behavior with friends, what's going on inside of us?

_____
_____
_____
_____

3. What's the best way for us to overcome our fear and our pride?

_____
_____
_____
_____

4. How do you feel when you praise others or call attention to the accomplishments of your friends?

_____
_____
_____
_____

Questions:

1. FEAR or PRIDE… Which one do you think is the bigger turn-off for people and why?

_____
_____
_____
_____
_____
_____

2. FEAR or PRIDE… Which one of these two emotions traps you most often, and what's your plan to be more REAL?

_____
_____
_____
_____
_____
_____
_____
_____

"You cannot get hurt by something you don't say."

31

The Boomerang Effect

Learning Objective:

You will understand service on behalf of others and what it produces.

Once upon a time there was a man who was very good at looking out for himself. He never concerned himself with others. He figured they could take care of themselves.

One night he had a dream where he saw a huge banquet table covered with delicious food. The entire table was overflowing with all his favorite foods, and he was hungry! Many of his friends and neighbors were there too. He was ready to start eating when he realized that all the forks and spoons were three feet long! They had such long handles that he couldn't get the food to his mouth.

As he looked around, this was true for all the guests at the table. No one could eat the food on their own plate. It seemed like this was someone's idea of a cruel prank.

Then he remembered something a wise man once said: "You can have anything you want if you help enough other people get what they want." He saw the hungry and frustrated look on a man's face across from him, so he picked up his long handled fork, scooped up some food from the man's plate, and fed him from across the table.

The man got such a smile on his face that it made him feel good about what he had done. So he decided to serve the woman sitting next to that man.

Pretty soon people started feeding each other from both sides of the table using the long forks until everyone had been given what they needed, including him. All the guests were happy and talking about the great banquet. The man thought it was the best meal he had ever eaten, and never once did he concern himself with what he wanted – only with what he could serve to others.

When the man woke up, he went out for a walk to think about this dream. As he strolled through the park, he saw a boy throwing a boomerang. With each throw the boomerang would fly out in a big arc and eventually come right back to the boy. Suddenly the meaning of the dream became clear:

"Whatever you give away comes back to you." He realized that if he wanted patience from others he needed first to give it away. If he wanted respect, he must first show respect. If he wanted kindness, he should give some to others; and eventually it would come back to him.

He realized that up until that moment he had been doing the exact opposite in his life. The decision was made. From now on he would pay attention to how he could help others get what they needed, and trust that gift to boomerang back to him. And in the process, the joy he felt in his dream was available to him every single day.

DISCUSSION:

1. What does the phrase "service to others" mean to you?

_____

_____

_____

_____

_____

2. What is the opposite of "service to others?"

_____

_____

_____
_____
_____

3. What causes that attitude or behavior?

_____
_____
_____
_____
_____

4. How do you feel when you get your eyes off yourself and care for the needs of others?

_____
_____
_____
_____
_____

Questions:

1. What examples have you seen in your experience of people serving others or caring for the needs of others?

_____
_____
_____
_____
_____
_____
_____

2. In what situations of your life could you do a better job of serving others? For whom? When? Where?

_____
_____
_____
_____
_____
_____
_____

"What goes around comes around."

32

Relating To Others

Communications – Fight or Flight

Learning Objective:

You will learn effective and ineffective methods of healthy dialogue with others.

W hat if I told you there's one thing you do every day that has a huge impact on each of your relationships, and yet you've never been taught how to do it well? This one skill can help you get along with supervisors, teachers, coaches, parents, spouses, and friends...and the sooner you learn it, the nicer people will treat you wherever you go.

I'm talking about the art of healthy conversations. Think about it… some conversations are positive and they bring people closer together. But some conversations go south in a hurry, leaving people feeling frustrated, or hurt, and sometimes angry. In each case, conversation skill, or lack of skill, is the single biggest factor that determines how we get along with others. Let's take a look at what's going on in your conversations.

Good relationships need good conversations. When a relationship doesn't feel very healthy, it's probably because the conversations aren't healthy. We can improve relationships when we improve our conversations, even if we don't communicate exactly the same way.

To do this we must understand what a healthy conversation looks like. It exists in the middle between two unhealthy extremes. One of them is called "Conversation Fight." It's a form of *verbal violence*.

The other is called "Conversation Flight." It's a kind of *verbal silence*. It usually begins when someone tries to begin a lecture or dominates a conversation by trying to control it. This usually gives way to name calling and attacking. It sounds like:

- You should have.

- You're supposed to.

- What's wrong with you?

- Here's what you need to do.

- You are such a _____.

- You are wrong.

In the other direction, people start to hide information. They start to withhold all their feelings and facts; and, if they pursue this a little further, pretty soon they withdraw completely.

Talk to the hands, the ears aren't listening. One word answers like "yup," "nope,'" and "maybe" are common along with crossed arms and no eye contact. These kinds of conversations just don't work. So how can we fix it?

Well, imagine a pool of information like a little swimming pool in the middle of a conversation. Into that pool you are invited to contribute your facts, your feelings, and your opinions. You get to add all that to the pool as long as you are not trying to control the pool. And then, of course, you must allow others to do the same thing.

If you don't want your conversation to look and feel like this, then work a lot harder to avoid *Conversation Flight* and *Conversation Fight*.

So here's the challenge. For the next week pay attention to your conversations. Be aware of when you head toward FIGHT or toward FLIGHT. Do your best to add your information to the conversation pool without trying to control the outcome. And then just see how well you get along with everyone in your life.

DISCUSSION:

1. How can you tell when you've had a really good conversation with someone?

_____
_____
_____
_____
_____

2. What is it like when a conversation doesn't go well. Describe the ingredients.

_____
_____
_____
_____
_____

3. Why do some people give lectures while others tend to clam up and withdraw?

_____
_____
_____
_____
_____

4. How should people learn more about the skills of healthy conversations?

_____

_____

_____

_____

_____

Questions:

1. What are the signs of disrespect creeping into a conversation, and why does it usually ruin the dialogue?

_____

_____

_____

_____

_____

_____

_____

2. In what situations could you do a better job of adding to the pool of information without trying to control the outcome? With whom?

_____

_____

_____

_____

_____

_____

_____

"Wise men speak because they have something to say. Fools speak because they want to say something."

33

Relating To Others

Villains and Victims

Learning Objective:

You will learn how to avoid turning people into Villains, and thinking like a Victim.

In our last lesson we discovered that conversations don't go very well when we choose *Verbal flight* or *Verbal fight*. Now let's look at why we get trapped in those behaviors and what we can do about it.

When conversations don't go well, it's usually because of one of two particular mistakes. The first mistake is when we think of others as *Villains*. In other words, we see them in our mind as the "bad guy." And, of course, if they are the bad guy we can treat them any way we want.

The other possibility is when we think of ourselves as *Victims*. "Oh, poor me. This is unfair. This shouldn't happen to me." As soon as we see ourselves as victims we are setting ourselves up for a different problem. What's the solution?

Well, it all comes down to asking ourselves a couple of key questions. We can have better conversations when we think of others as just normal people who make mistakes. And we can get there if we ask ourselves, "I wonder why a normal person would behave like this?" Wondering is the first key to considering the possibility that there is a reason behind another person's activities.

And, of course, when we look at ourselves openly and honestly, we should ask ourselves the questions, "I wonder what part of this activity belongs to me?" and "I wonder where I'm at fault." As soon as we realize that, we can stop seeing ourselves as Victims and seeing other people as Villains.

This opens the door for us to experience the three ingredients of great conversations and great relationships:

1. Find common ground. What do we both want in this situation? In what areas do we agree?

2. Demonstrate mutual respect with words, tone, and body language, no matter what.

3. Reach a mutual understanding. Strive to understand each other, even when you can't agree.

Great conversations lead to great relationships, but it requires people who are committed to assuming the very best about each other.

DISCUSSION:

1. What does it mean to "label" someone? Why do we do it?

_____

_____

_____

_____

2. How do we treat people after we give them a negative label?

_____

_____

_____

_____

3. How have you felt when you've been labeled by someone?

_____

_____

_____

_____

Questions:

1. What causes you to turn someone into a "Villain" in your mind? When do you think of yourself as a "Victim?"

_____
_____
_____
_____
_____
_____

2. In what situation could you have a better conversation with a particular person in your life? What are you going to do about it?

_____
_____
_____
_____
_____
_____

"You don't know the story unless you are the story."

34

Relating To Others

Mission: Sacrifice

Learning Objective:

You will understand personal Sacrifice and putting others first.

O nly in baseball will you find a term that represents one of the greatest qualities found in humans. I'm talking about the "Sacrifice." The Sacrifice Bunt, or the Sacrifice Fly, is used to improve the position of another player on the team by letting yourself be put out. What a concept! Now here's a real life example.

An American professional tennis player won three Grand Slam titles, ranking him among the best tennis players in the world. He was also the first African American ever to win the singles title at Wimbledon, the US Open, and the Australian Open. But what most people don't know is that none of that would have ever happened had it not been for the Sacrifice of his older brother who was serving in the Vietnam War.

The US Military had a policy that prevented more than one son from the same family from serving at the same time. After his brother finished his first tour in Vietnam, his younger brother was suddenly in danger of being sent to Vietnam.

Without telling his brother, he volunteered to serve a second tour of Vietnam so that his brother could stay home and continue his tennis career. Only their father was told the truth. To sacrifice something of value for another person's good is the highest level of serving. It requires taking your eyes off yourself and being more concerned about someone else.

Where are you willing to make a Sacrifice to meet the needs of others? Who are you willing to put ahead of yourself today?

DISCUSSION:

1. What does it mean to sacrifice something for another person?

_____

_____

_____

_____

2. What examples of personal Sacrifice have you witnessed?

_____

_____

_____

_____

3. How do most people react when they realize someone has put their needs first?

_____

_____

_____

_____

4. Why don't more people sacrifice for others?

_____

_____

_____

_____

Questions:

1. What personal qualities do you see in people who make sacrifices for others? What do you admire most?

_____
_____
_____
_____
_____
_____

2. Who has made significant personal Sacrifices for you during your life? When? How do you feel about it?

_____
_____
_____
_____
_____
_____

"It's better to give than receive."

35

Relating To Others

Other People's Mistakes

Learning Objective:

You will learn to understand the choice of two possible responses to the mistakes of others.

People make mistakes, say the wrong thing, or sometimes just forget what's important. We have a choice about how we respond to them when this happens. Some of our behaviors cause additional hurt and, if done consistently, destroy our relationship with them. Other options strengthen relationships by lifting people up and building upon their potential greatness.

How do we react to other people's mistakes? We may choose what we call **The Three C's**:

1. To Criticize

2. To Complain

3. To Condemn

It's only human to make mistakes, and a better choice is to choose what we call The Three E's:

1. To Encourage

2. To Educate

3. To Enjoy

The Three C's, or the Three E's - it's your choice.

DISCUSSION:

1. What kind of a response do you usually get when you criticize someone's efforts or mistakes?

_____

_____

_____

_____

_____

2. What is the purpose of complaining about things done by others?

_____

_____

_____
_____
_____

3. How is it possible to "educate" someone without sounding like a "know-it-all"?

_____
_____
_____
_____
_____

4. Explain what it means to "enjoy" someone – even if they've messed up.

_____
_____
_____
_____
_____

Questions:

1. Why do experts say that the 3 C's are the fastest way to destroy relationships?

_____

_____

_____

_____

_____

_____

_____

2. Describe situations in which you have used the 3 E's in your friendships or family and what impact it has had.

_____

_____

_____

_____

_____

_____

_____

"Praise publicly, criticize privately."

36

The Final Secret To Thrive

Learning Objective:

You will review the **Power of Four, You Are Alive 2 Thrive,** and know where to find answers to future questions.

Congratulations! You've completed the *Power of Four* lessons. We began this book by calling it a journey. That means that while you've completed the lessons, the journey will go on and on. And that's really great news! You don't want to stop learning now!

You've been given the fundamentals in four areas:

- Knowing Me
- Managing Me
- Understanding Others
- Relating to Others

This is **The Power of Four**.

Your mind has been expanded in each of these areas just by listening to the messages. And if you put the lessons into action, you've grown and matured more than you realize. Now you know yourself better and are more aware of how you think and react. You're able to guide your thoughts in more positive directions each day.

You've learned how to understand and accept others who are different than you. And you're ready to build stronger friendships, as well as meet the needs of others.

You were valuable when you started this book; but because of the things you've learned, you're now more likely to add value to every situation you run into, and to every person you meet. By being willing to learn, you've put yourself into a special group of people who are becoming more of who they are meant to be, so they can contribute more, and enjoy life more.

Now here's the final secret. Everything taught in **You Are Alive 2 Thrive** is available to you through some common resources: books, videos, and other people! The answers you seek to life's greatest challenges can be found if you're willing to open your mind. You'll find things that inspire you, push you, and some things you'll disagree with. The stories and the research found in books, and listening to the new ideas and the opinions of other people can save you from learning the long, slow, painful way of trial and error.

Here's a promise I can make to you. The books you read and the people you meet will shape your life forever... because a mind stretched by an idea can never return to its original shape. Keep an open mind when talking with people. Practice **The Power of Four**, and keep on learning!

Win the biggest game – LIFE. You don't get a second chance!

DISCUSSION:

1. Why was "**You Are Live 2 Thrive**" created for you?

_____

_____

_____

_____

_____

2. What would be the benefit of re-reading your answers from earlier lessons?

_____

_____

_____

_____
_____

3. What's the single most important lesson you
remember from "**You Are Live 2 Thrive**"?

_____
_____
_____
_____
_____
_____

Questions:

1. What is the most important or meaningful book you have read? What did you learn?

_____

_____

_____

_____

_____

_____

_____

2. What situation, issue, or challenge in your life might be helped by finding the right book? Do you know where to look?

_____

_____

_____

_____

_____

_____

_____

Joe's Sayings

Through my many years of experience I have collected a number of sayings that have been meaningful to me. Here are a few I'd like to share with you.

Health

"It is health that is the real wealth, not pieces of gold."

"The best and most efficient pharmacy is within your own system."

"It's all about the plumbing; keep it clean and strong and live long."

"Growing old is mandatory, growing up is optional."

Achievement

"Practice the 3 P's: Pleasant, Personable, Persistent."

"Study while others are sleeping; work while others are loafing; prepare while others are playing; and dream while others are wishing."

"Winners do what losers don't want to do."

"It's amazing what you can accomplish if you don't care who gets the credit."

"A goal without a plan is just a wish."

Character

"Character is doing something right even when no one is looking."

"Take care of your reputation. It is your most valuable asset."

Wisdom

"Turn your wounds into wisdom."

"Don't repeat anything you wouldn't sign your name to."

"Wisdom is wasted on the old if not passed onto the young."

Education

"If you think education is expensive, try ignorance."

"A child educated only in school is an uneducated child."

"Educate yourself about yourself; learn to know and like yourself."

Luck

"Luck is when preparation meets opportunity."

"Luck never made a person wise."

Memories

"Memories are the key, not to the past but to the future."

"It's surprising how much of memory is built around things unnoticed at the time."

Spirituality

"It doesn't matter what you believe, only that you are a good person."

"Life is not measured by the number of breaths we take, but by the moments that take our breath away."

"Don't expect to build up the weak by pulling down the strong."

Family

"Families are like fudge; mostly sweet with a few nuts."

Marriage

"Marriage is the will of two to make one."

"Don't smother each other. No one can grow in the shade."

"A successful marriage requires falling in love many times with the same person."

"Marriage requires physical attraction, common interests, and values and the best possible communication."

Children

"The best inheritance a parent can give to his children is a few minutes of his time each day."

"When you teach your son, you teach your son's son."

"Don't handicap your children by making their lives easy."

"Children are our most valuable resource and the best hope for the future."

"Live so that when your children think of fairness and integrity, they think of you."

"Anyone can be a Mommy or Daddy, but it takes someone special to be a parent."

Friends

"Your friends love you for who you are, not what you have."

"Friends are relatives that you pick yourself."

Leadership

"Leaders praise loudly and blame softly."

"Lead, follow, or get out of the way."

Happiness

"Happiness is knowing who you are and living life the way you want."

"Refrain from envy; it is the source of much unhappiness."

Self-Esteem

"Nothing builds self-esteem and self-confidence like accomplishments."

Attitude

"We all have good qualities; look for yours."

"To be beautiful means to be yourself. You don't need to be accepted by others."

"What you think, you become."

Courage and Risk

"Courage is being scared and still doing the right thing."

"Courage is what it takes to stand up and speak; courage is also what it takes to sit down and listen."

"Life's greatest risk is never daring to risk."

Giving

"Make a living by what you get; make a life by what you give."

"Don't mistake kindness for weakness."

"I will give a hand up, not a handout."

Work

"Do what you like and you will never work a day in your life."

"One today is worth two tomorrows; don't leave 'til tomorrow what you can do today."

"You can't build a reputation on what you are planning to do."

Money

"Money is a terrible master but a great servant."

"It's easy to make a buck; it's harder to make a difference."

"Just remember the gold; he who has the gold makes the rules."

"Learn how to be a member of the SKI club! (Spend the Kids' Inheritance),"

"A rich person has good health, family and good friends."

In Closing

I hope you enjoyed going through the 36 lessons. I also hope that, in the process, you had a few AHA moments that will change your life.

If you can master these 36 lessons and become proficient, I can assure you that you will be ALIVE TO THRIVE. This is not going to be easy, and from time to time you will likely slip back. However, now that you have the foundation, you have a much better chance.

The only thing that would be better than your learning these lessons now would be that you would have learned them earlier in life. The real solution would be to provide early learning to children starting at birth.

To that end, my foundation is dedicated to being an advocate for our government to spend our money wisely and invest in our most precious asset - our children, by funding early learning resource centers for all children from the ages from birth to 5. These centers will focus on health, social and emotional learning, and academics. They will also help mothers and fathers become the best parents they can be. Please sign declaration referred to on page 188 to help with this cause.

All profits made from this book will go to that cause!

For those of you who have purchased my book, and taken the time to read it, I would like to make a donation in your honor. If you feel that this book has value and would like to help others, I will donate books in your honor to any school or organization that has 501(c)(3) status.

All you have to do is present the book to an instructor who will agree to teach these 36 lessons to people who can benefit.

With the purchase of this book you will have access to all the online life-changing educational videos on the SantoroFoundation.org website. To register, just use the code:

2BSELF

And, finally, please share your thoughts with me and remember:

"Wisdom is wasted on the old,
if not passed on to the young."

Joe@SantoroFoundation.org

The Declaration

We the people of the United States, in order to accomplish the next Great American Achievement, demand that OUR government cut the waste in spending, use those funds for early learning and spend OUR money wisely by investing 3% of the federal budget in our most precious asset: ALL OUR CHILDREN.

We are asking the government to invest in high quality preschool and child care for all children ages 0 to 5. Early learning professionals would also help mothers and fathers learn how to become the best parents they can be by offering high quality at home education support, online learning tools, and center based programs.

These centers would be owned and operated by the private sector, but measured, monitored, and rated by a third party to ensure excellence. This program should focus on social and emotional intelligence, health, and academics. We believe the 3% investment will yield a 5-18% return (ROI). The 3% investment would not be funded by increasing taxes, but by reducing excessive waste, and prioritizing and eliminating some existing programs that do not benefit us as Americans.

Changing how we educate our children, we will start to build the foundation that we need to improve how we think about ourselves, and how we relate to others. This foundation will provide the basis to help ALL CHILDREN become the best they can be, and to become responsible adults.

Please sign this declaration by going to www.acffnow.org and clicking on "Declaration".

I Would Appreciate Your Opinion and Help

Positive book reviews greatly affect how a book is presented on Amazon. If you found this book to be helpful and believe it's worth sharing, would you please take a few moments to write a short review.

 Just go to the Amazon book site, click on "customer reviews" and then "add a review". Add your rating and a short review (could be just one sentence or as long as you want) and you are done. It only takes a short while, and it will help me to help others.

All profits from this book go directly to the Santoro Education Lifeskills Foundation.

All my best and thank you so much for reading **"You Are Alive 2 Thrive?"**

Joe Santoro

Made in the USA
Columbia, SC
11 November 2018